An Eagle's Flight
In Poetry

An Eagle's Flight

In Poetry

by
Edmond E. Frank

Copyright 2021
by Edmond E. Frank

All rights reserved. No part of this book may be reproduced by any means or in any form without the express permission of the author.

ISBN 978-1-7348367-8-3

Dedication

I've spent a great deal of my life
pissing into the face of God.
God needs no apology.
All God needs is that we live our lives
the very best we can.
We are the part of God that experiences it.
And me?
All I need do, is to appreciate my life.
And I do—
Most of all, I appreciate Life's Spiritual Laws.
In the light of which I am privileged to see
a different perspective of life—the real truth.
It is a light in which some refuse to look.

This book is dedicated to

Shawna

She was my perfect love. I was not hers. Yet, for me, true love—once given—stands immortal.

Quote

Those living a lie will unconsciously seek validation. Those living a lie consciously, will fight to the death for its truth. Those living the truth don't give a rat's ass what you believe.

Redneck Spirituality—Book Three

Table of Contents

The Poetry from the Original Manuscript
Of *The Soul of an Eagle*

NOTE:
No poetry was written for Chapters 11, 13, 15, 32, 33, or 34.

Original Prologue
    2   *Life Is About the Ride*

Inescapable Sentiment—Ch 1
    6   *No Free Lunches*
    9   *The Flavors of Selfishness*

Masquerading Love—Ch 2
    12   *Taking It With Me*
    14   *Magnets*

It's Not the Money, Only the Price—Ch 3
    18   *Feelings*

The Finger of God—Ch 4
    20   *Naked Soul*

Ten Thousand Feet—Ch 5
    22   *Ten Thousand Feet*

Steer on the Kill Floor—Ch 6
    26   *Here . . . Now*
    28   *A Nurturing Woman*
    29   *The First Step*
    31   *Always*

Oh, Cheesus—Ch 7

- 34 Castles
- 36 Pretending
- 37 Absence
- 38 Next To Me
- 40 Babel
- 43 By Your Example
- 45 Extraordinary People
- 46 I know Your Tears

The Battlefield of Unmet Dreams—Ch 8

- 50 The Dream
- 51 Inner Quest... The Seminar
- 53 Surrendering to You
- 54 To Be...

Flash Floods of Life—Ch 9

- 56 Tigers
- 59 What He Heard You Say
- 60 Bridges
- 61 I Have To Be Right
- 62 Mirrors

Have Mercy Baby—Chapter 10

- 66 Mercy Fuck
- 67 Loving, Cheating, and Leaving
- 68 Mourning

Best of Times in the Worst of Times—Ch 11

❖ *No poetry written in this chapter*

Is Love Such a Hard Thing to Swallow?—Ch 12
- 70   *Sex*
- 72   *Reflections*
- 73   *Are You The One?*
- 75   *Goodbye Letter*

The Saga of Doc—Ch 13
❖ *No poetry written in this chapter*

Doc's Chicken Exit—Ch 14
- 78   *The Truth About Friends*

Shopping at the Meat Market—Ch 15
❖ No poetry written in this chapter

Eagle Quest—Ch 16
- 82   *Teressa Nichole Travon*
- 83   *One Last Step*
- 84   *Eagle Quest One Seminar*
- 86   *Challenge of the Soul Mate*
- 88   *Challenge Eagle*

Single . . . Available . . . . Women—Ch 17
- 90   *Regina*
- 92   *Pendulum Swings*
- 94   *You . . . So Beautiful You*
- 97   *Move In*

Hard Hearts Sometimes Break—Ch 18
- 100   *Righteous*
- 102   *Judging You*
- 103   *Mom . . . Dad*

Protecting That Inner Child—Ch 19
- 106 Heirloom
- 108 New Mommy
- 109 Of Shoelaces, Trust, & Self-esteem

Thirty Days Babe—Ch 20
- 116 Eagle Quest Two
- 120 Broken Promises and Lies
- 123 Carpe Diem
- 125 Shark Bite

Burying the Past—Ch 21
- 128 Sir Knight
- 129 Do Eagles Always Soar Alone?
- 131 Farewell My Love
- 133 Dawn

Motorcycle Wheels and Macho Balls—Ch 22
- 136 Sparring With the Dinosaur
- 140 Fears
- 141 The Snuggle
- 142 Passions
- 145 Perceptions
- 147 Judgment

Ka-Bar—Chapter 23
- 150 Memorial Day

Life Changes and Remains the Same—Ch 24
- 152 Burger Barn
- 155 Forgive Me My Love

Painting Pink Turds—Ch 25
    169   *Leasha*

Riding a Bad Assed Machine—Ch 26
    162   *In the Wind*
    164   *Sedona*
    168   *A Cry in the Silence*

Lessons, Tests, & Validations—Ch 27
    170   *The Correction*
    171   *Loving Lucy*
    172   *Best Friends*

Once in the Eclipse of a Blue Moon—Ch 28
    176   *Eclipse of the Blue Moon*

The Ghost of Durango Calling—Ch 29
    180   *My Memory of You*
    184   *What Was It Calling Me?*

Moose Milk & Horse Puckies—Ch 30
    190   *Is She the One?*
    192   *A Place Called Loving*

Loving Mona—Ch 31
    194   *The One Who Won't Leave*
    195   *Maureen*
    197   *Florence*

The Correction Always Goes >HERE< —Ch 32
    ❖ No poetry written in this chapter

Goes Where?—Ch 33
❖ No poetry written in this chapter

No Correction Needed—Ch 34
❖ No poetry written in this chapter

Epilogue
    200   *Gifts*
    201   *There's A Wind*

About the Author

Acknowledgments

The memoir novel *The Courage of a Butterfly* and its sequel were a labor of love, on-and-off for over 25 years. It could be said they were the school ground for this writer's ability to write. Over the years there have been numerous teachers scattered throughout the various critique groups, and even some at the university. It would be great if I could remember and acknowledge them all by name—but I can't. They are important to this book of poetry only in that poems were written into both the original manuscript of, *The Courage of a Butterfly*, and this, the sequel novel, *Soul of an Eagle*. Nearly all who critiqued those novels begged me to take the poems out. I eventually agreed. They said it would be as speed bumps to the story—they said. Speed bumps, or just shitty poetry—you decide. Authors see their work as perfect. I only know they came from my heart.

I wish to thank *the Aliante Writers Critique Group, the Sin City Writers Group, the Henderson Writers Group, and the 5Artz Writer's Workshop at Barns and Noble, Summerlin.*

Many in these four groups are published and all are excellent writers. They have been the most supportive to me. With the other critique groups, there was always the fact that many of the members were not of this venue—Self-Help, Spirituality, New Age, New Thought—and felt the need to critique the thought system and not so much the writing. Those mentioned here were open-minded and supportive.

There are my beta readers:
Betty Hart
LillyWhelband

And my editor and good friend Karen Diehl. The excellence of her work makes mine sound intelligent—sometimes.

There is Joylynn Ross of Pathtopublishing.com.
Joylynn is another friend and mentor—and is an expert in the publishing industry.

Lastly, there is Bobby of Bobby Daniels Graphics, my cover designer. Probable the most important person in influencing you, the reader, to buy this book, he is a true artist. I highly recommend him to other writers.

Poetry is the language of emotion, and emotions are the words of the soul. As such, there is always poetic license for those who are emotional wrecks in life. Without it, no doubt this poet would have crashed and burned in that long ago time when most of this was written. Certainly, if I had not heard the messages authored here by my soul, I would not have survived.

Then there are the beautiful souls of the various people—mostly women—who love me, and I, them.

Life is empty until you take it to "GRATEFUL." It is the elixir that fills you—it is the sacrament of life.

Introduction
(Shared in part with *The Courage of a Butterfly Poetry Book*)

These poems were originally distributed throughout *Soul of an Eagle*—the Sequel Novel of *The Courage of a Butterfly*. They were immersed as part of the story. But for those who don't like poetry, they were just confusing bumps in the road of life—bumps that couldn't be skipped—and could send the reader into a skid.

So what was the story line—and what was I, a redneck, doing writing poetry? Was I just staring into the headlights to even offer it up.

You might say it started with me in a hospital facing my imminent death. There is a presence that permeated an ICU. Some call it the presence of Death, some The Grim Reaper, and some just know it as The Angel (of Death).

In my own way, I met The Angel—knew him intimately. You see, you just can't tell that Angel the same lies you've been telling yourself throughout your life—the ones that allowed you to get out of bed every morning and go about your life.

If you ever stopped telling them to yourself—and pretending to believe—you would die. You see, when you change your mind, your beliefs about anything, your whole life changes. The old one stops—just dies—and a new one begins.

What holds us all from telling ourselves the truth is the price we'd have to pay to acknowledge it. With me, that price was my wife. I loved her so deeply and for so long that I could not—no, make that *would not*—admit the truth. I was her security in life, but I was *never* the love of her life.

Thing was, for me to lie to The Angel at that point, would have definitely cost me my life—*my physical life*. I got honest and it did cost me my wife and everything else that then was of importance to me. The price was worth it. In the process I discovered the Spiritual Laws. They are merely those common-sense things that, like the Law of Gravity, always hold true.

As I see it, the law of gravity is a physical law that was set down for this universe by its Creator. Like any law it always holds true. As that Creator actually is it all, the entire universe, then I, myself, being a part of this universe, am an actual part of God. It could be said we, each person, are as a drop in the vast Ocean of God.

And me? Like DNA, I have it all—all the power I can possibly wield in the creation of my life. And to that point, I wielded it poorly. I did not like, respect, or even accept that person I was. As such, I was pissing into the face of God.

Life—All of it—from what we eat to what we excrete; IT IS ALL GOD. Yeah, I know. Now I'm sounding like some religious zealot standing on a street corner raving.

Except, MY sign doesn't say: "REPENT! THE WORLD IS COMING TO AN END!"

No. My sign says: "Open the eyes of your mind, see the truth—AND LIVE IT!"

So now, back to my statement: *"Life—all of it—IS ALL GOD."*

You know how a fish doesn't't know water until they're out of it—immersed in the air? Well despite what Organized Religions would have you believe, you don't need to go to church to find God. You are an actual part and piece of Him/Her/It. If you want to find God, look within yourself—but LOOK with the truth. The truth is the Spiritual Laws.

I discovered those laws, and with them I looked. Much of what came out of me was then poetry—this poetry. Me! This big tattooed, motorcycle riding, wrench turning fucking redneck mechanic. Yeah, I excreted it. It's ALL about life—about the TRUTH of it—AND IT'S ALL GOD.

The Poetry

❖ **AGAIN, PLEASE NOTE:**
Several chapters are missing because no poetry was written for them in the original manuscript.

Prologue

2 An Eagle's Flight—In Poetry

Life Is About the Ride

When you see that bike,
the joy it gives to your life . . .
Despite all,
you know you must ride.
It's a part of you,
not to know, just to do . . .
Life is about the ride.

When you look at that bike,
the power, the beauty,
the magnificence inside,
unleashed only when you ride.
It's not where you've been,
nor where you will be,
life is only about the ride.

It's the wind in your face . . .
though it's with death that you race,
you've no need or desire to hide.
When you're loving and living
the best part of life,
Life is always about the ride.

Wind blows `cross the coals of your soul,
fanning them brightly aglow.
Though the wind may be cold,
in their warmth you are whole.
Your world is lit by what is inside,
When your life is about the ride.

4 An Eagle's Flight—In Poetry

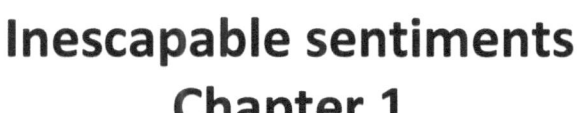

Inescapable sentiments
Chapter 1

No Free Lunches

To receive, I have to give.
For anything I get,
there is a price to be paid . . .
For the Universe always balances.
The trick is in the knowing . . .
in seeing the price,
and in being willing to pay.
I loved a woman . . .
beautiful . . . sensuous . . . exquisite . . .
and wanted her company . . .
forever.
Yet, had not the wisdom . . .
the maturity to see the price.
For the price was the ownership of my life.
I gave her the power . . .
the authority . . .
the control over me.
And in the doing, lay the real price . . .
the respect I held for myself.
On that higher, unconscious level . . .
I knew . . .

*the price was too high.
And inside I held an anger . . .
not of her . . .
Rather, directed inside . . .
for paying the price . . .
for being disloyal to my soul.
Until came the day I awakened . . .
became conscious . . .
and understood.
The day I took my power back . . .
gathered my self esteem.
Defaulted the loan of her acceptance.
Her demands then became angry . . .
Angry demands of payment . . .
payment for her company.
And then . . .
as must be, we parted.
In gaining my freedom,
the cost I paid?
I will bear a sorrow in my soul,
a sorrow which is forever.
And again, a price, a cost I did not see . . .*

The respect . . .
and acceptance of my parents.
And the knowledge . . .
unwanted knowledge . . .
that their love was always conditional.
Yes, when you get, you have to give.
There is a price for everything received.
In this life there are no free lunches.
Yet, to truly live, following my heart,
living as it guides me.
Not in what is good or bad . . .
Rather, what is loving . . .
for loving is what works for me.
Such, is to know an ecstasy
in the core of my very being,
that I have never known . . .
before.

The Flavors of Selfishness

This is your life . . .
only you can live it.
As such, it is the nature . . .
a universal law of Mankind . . .
always . . . to be selfish.
Yet selfish is always tasted
in one of two flavors.
Flavor one is in living your life
to its highest joy . . .
following your heart in truly living . . .
and truly loving yourself.
Being all that you can be . . .
for you.
Flavor two is living your life
the way you were taught.
Following blindly,
asleep to your heart.
Living your life for them.
Living a set of rules . . . beliefs . . .
not necessarily truths.

10 An Eagle's Flight—In Poetry

Some didn't work . . .
for them.
Nor allow any joy . . .
in you.
Then expecting your progeny to do . . .
as you.
To validate your misery . . .
after you.
You have a choice . . .
right here . . . right now.
Pick one!

Masquerading Love
Chapter 2

Taking It With Me

What is my want?
What is my need?
My meaning . . .
what do I gain from this life?
Is it that my home be a mansion,
high on a hill above . . .
overlooking others?
Is it my car be the finest . . .
the fastest . . .
the most beautiful?
Do these toys I buy, or the fun I take,
provide purpose to my life?
Yes, attaining of things seems a joy to me.
Yet, once gotten, soon pales with time.
For it's not possessing the thing,
it remains here when I'm gone.
It is the growth I get when I strive . . .
the truth I find beneath the lies.

*Yes growth . . . and truth . . .
that is the reality . . .
the joy for me.
That intangible reality
I'll take with me
when time comes . . .
to be leaving this life.
The joy of growth
beneath this eagle's wing,
is the wind that makes me soar.
And the growth of my soul
is the only thing I can take . . .
when I soar over.*

Magnets

Opposites attract . . .
Yes, the male pole—me,
attracts the female pole—you . . .
Like a magnet, opposite poles attract . . .
opposite forces connect together.
And yet, just so . . .
it is always the same poles
that point the same direction . . .
to the place they want to be together.
To the poles of the earth
the magnet will turn . . .
point to what is reality.
Just so, in life . . .
those going through life together,
staying connected on their journey . . .
always have the same attractions . . .
are pointed to and going for . . .
the same dreams.
Should one's force change . . .
grow in another direction,
then will either's will . . .
either's arms . . .
be strong enough to hold?

For two hearts will always grow together . .
or they will grow apart.
We are only together on this journey of life,
on the pathway of our hearts . . .
when sharing the same dreams.
When each ones pathway, in the now,
is attracted by the same future.
We travel together in mutual support,
supplying each other's needs.
In times of weakness
when one's heart is heavy . . .
the other helps carry along.
The growth of the soul
is the force that propels
the energy that fuels our dreams.
Should one's heart quit growing
the other may try towing . . .
pulling at them, to come along.
Then with tears in their eyes,
they watch it all die . . .
when the energy . . .
the attraction . . .
is gone.

16 An Eagle's Flight—In Poetry

It's Not the Money—Only the Price
Chapter 3

Feelings

I am responsible for my feelings . . .
my beliefs . . . my deeds in life.
You . . . for yours.
How you think about me
is not my concern . . .
only how I think about you.
For it is always a reflection of me,
that I see . . . in you.

The Finger of God
Chapter 4

Naked Soul

She was a beautiful woman . . .
a loving . . .
open soul.
She held no mask out
to hide behind . . .
no pretense to the world.
She showed up in life in truth . . .
the naked truth of who she was.
This beautiful . . . this loving . . .
this naked open soul.
She knew who she was . . .
she'd looked within.
And wanted a man of courage . . .
for she expected the same . . .
of him.

Ten Thousand Feet
Chapter 5

Ten Thousand Feet

Ten thousand feet, the distance between . . .
Separating, determining my beliefs . . .
my feelings . . .
My acceptance of me.
Changing my mind
for the rest of my life.

Ten thousand feet, at 120 miles per hour,
The distance I'll cover at the speed it takes . . .
to make my choice.
Will I live my life in courage?
Or spend it dying . . .
in cowardice?

Ten thousand feet . . .
and forty seconds.
The time it takes right here—right now . . .
to fly thru my fear . . .
or fall back into . . .
my cowardice.

Ten thousand feet . . .
The question is not: "Will?"
Will I live?
Will I die?
The question is . . .
"How?"

24 An Eagle's Flight—In Poetry

Like a Steer on the Kill Floor
Chapter 6

Here... Now

The past is gone . . .
no longer here.
The future is yet to be.
The only living is in the present,
in the here . . .
right now.
For my mind to dwell in
the sorrows or joys of the past,
is to be dead . . .
to be not alive.
Because I am alive in the now . . .
now is the only time there is.
And yet, there is a purpose
for my mind . . .
to often touch the past.
It provides insight, education . . .
what has worked . . .
what has not.
It provides a guide for my life . . .
in the here . . . for the now.
To touch the past is vital.
To dwell in the past is death.
And to often touch the future

*is also necessary . . . is vital . . .
to guide my life, here right now.
Where I want to be in the future
is a target for the gun-sight of my mind.
My future . . . my wants . . . my goals . . .
need to be often sighted in on,
and corrections made on my path,
here . . . and now.
For my mind to dwell in the future
is also death.
The future is tomorrow,
and tomorrow never comes . . .
Time spent dwelling in the future or past,
is time not lived . . . time lost . . .
lost forever from my life . . . now.
Time . . .
the only commodity granted me on birth.
I want to spend it wisely.
For I don't know its quantity . . .
I do know, that in the end,
it is not enough . . .
Its quality is up to me.
Here . . . now . . .*

A Nurturing Woman

A nurturing woman sees . . . gives . . .
not what she wants,
rather, what she sees I need.
Encouraging . . . uplifting . . . enabling . . .
those things that are of my heart,
without expectations . . . payments . . .
returns on her investment.
Giving love freely . . .
providing nourishment . . .
for the growth of my soul.
And in her giving . . . receiving . . .
growing with my love.

The First Step

Yes, I left you Dear . . .
to seek my spirituality . . .
to tread that pathway . . .
to journey within.
And though it is only within,
it still carries me away . . .
so far away . . . from you.
To stay with you, requires of you,
that you tread your pathway too.
For spirituality always seeks spirituality.
And as in any journey,
the path begins with just one step.
That first step . . . is choice.
Yours . . . mine . . .
I've made my choice.
Taken my first tottering steps . . .
Found awe in a glimpse . . .
of the beauty . . .

the magnificence . . .
within me . . .
and within you.
It is something . . .
would only I could . . .
know in me . . .
and share with you.
Yet the step . . .
the choice . . .
you must make it yourself.
It is a step only you can take . . .
freely . . . willingly . . .
courageously.

Always

You are my soul mate.
Yesterday I heard you say,
I want you here . . . with me . . . always.
"Always?" I ask.
For "always" means expectations.
Expectations for me to be . . .
then, like now . . . who you want.
Yes . . . you are who I want . . . now.
We are soul mates.
For I know your soul . . .
It is like unto mine.
I know your thoughts . . .
even before you say them.
Like me, I know those even you don't say,
and I know those you will do.
For right here . . . right now . . .
we are soul mates . . .
you and I.
In just being with you,
right here . . . right now . . .
I can grow . . .
I can learn so much,
about what I don't see in me.

And yet, the constant in the Universe . . .
remember, is change.
Change in you . . . change in me.
Yes, we will change . . . both will grow.
That you will still be there . . .
Still want to be there . . .
In that moment of then . . . depends.
For we will grow together . . .
or we will grow apart . . .
as we follow our hearts.
Conscious minds want to grow together . . .
be there . . .
always
even comes the time our hearts are not.
'Twould never be in joy.
For joy is where your heart is . . .
always.
My hope for you . . .
my intent for me . . .
is to live in joy . . .
always.
Then together . . . or apart . . .
I will know . . .
And I will love you . . .
always.

Oh, Cheesus
Chapter 7

Castles

Mankind is taught from the day of his birth
to deny himself . . .
To discount his worth to others . . .
To give his very life's blood
so that others might have . . .
To make them matter more than he.
And too . . .
he is taught the importance of modesty.
That 'tis a virtue to deny
the dreams of his life . . .
his possessions . . . his importance . . .
his fame.
More so . . .
he is taught to accept as his,
a belief system of what's right and wrong,
as believed in someone else's mind . . .
Rather than one that is based
on what works . . .
or what doesn't work for him.
He is taught that "righteous"
is solid and unchangeable.

These are a few of the beliefs that mold him
into becoming the man he will be.
They are the foundation of the house
he builds upon this earth . . .
the monument his life comes to mean.
It is the teaching of modesty
as a virtue of mind . . .
that limits him to a smallness in his
and limits the foundation of his house
with impossibly small building stones.
Yes . . .
a rock-solid, righteous . . .
modest foundation
can support a tract house for his life.
Never a castle for the grandeur
that is the magnificence in every man's soul.
To build that tract house into a castle,
is not possible with a modest mind.
His belief in himself is what limit his life,
Without seeing the grandeur of his soul
he cannot build a castle
to house it in this life.

Pretending

Every adult is really a child
pretending to be an adult.
For nearly all our beliefs about life . . .
about us . . .
were learned . . .
were formed . . .
as a child.
The places we go to within our minds
when the events of our life unfold,
is still the same . . .
now . . . as then.
With this adult . . . with that child.
Yet this adult tries to pretend . . .
it is different.

Absence

Dad . . . I never knew you . . .
nor you . . . me.
Did you ever want it to be?
No . . . I think not.
For if you had . . . you would . . .
and you could . . . yet . . .
you didn't.
Who were you then?
I never knew . . .
nor who you are right now.
This man . . . this mystery . . .
Could it possibly be,
that what you taught to me?
Was the reason . . . the why . . .
it took so long for me . . .
to know me?
And for me
to know my son . . .
and my son . . .
me?

The Next Me

Yes Son . . .
You are my legacy . . .
my gift to the world.
Would I want you to carry-on after me?
Have I taught you to be the next me?
No . . . I pray not . . . No!
For that me who raised you . . .
taught you your beliefs . . .
was the same as the one taught me . . .
I was never there for you . . .
Nor him . . . for me.
And too, yes . . .
I pray you can see . . .
Nor ever want to be . . .
the next me,
The me I was back then.
For the me that you now see . . .
can love himself . . . and you.
Would hold his baby to his breast . . .
nurture him with all his heart . . .
sing to . . . teach . . . and feed.

*And always be there.
Even change his fragrant diaper . . .
lovingly . . .
in full appreciation for the gifts
given from him . . . to me.
Yes . . . that me is the one
I would hope you could be . . .
Yet know it is not the one
you've seen in me.
Yet still . . .
for your son . . . and his . . . and his . . .
I hope it is the one you'll be . . .
and the one he'll want to . . .
and he'll want to . . .
and he'll want to . . .
be.*

Babel

Dad . . .
the thoughts . . . the beliefs . . .
you hold as truth in your mind . . .
about me.
The things I say or the things I do . . .
You will choose to hear, and to see . . .
through the hearing-aid of your paradigm . . .
the colored glasses covering
the eyes of your mind.
I can never be "right" with you
until you want me to . . .
by changing something about you . . .
about the way that you view me.
That view is colored by negativity.
A son neglecting . . .
shirking his responsibilities.
Incapable . . . unable . . .
to do life "right."
For "right" is the color you paint your life.

And yet . . .
can you not see
that for me?
This life is mine!
You cannot live it,
anymore than I . . .
can change your mind.
Dad . . .
those glasses you wear . . .
that you look at me thru . . .
are tinted with mistrust . . .
The light coming thru
looks incapable to you.
Yes, this is what you see
when you look at me . . .
The beliefs you choose
to view me through.
Why? What does it serve?
For it keeps us apart . . .
It keeps hurt in your heart . . .
and enables it in mine too.

*Is this the purpose
that is important to you?
Or is it simply that the things I do . . .
are things that you would not do.
Your beliefs about men . . .
your beliefs about God . . .
your beliefs about life . . .
say you can't.
If you'll accept that I do . . .
what does that say about you?
It says simply that your life . . .
your God . . . you . . .
are wrong!
Can you not see for you to accept me . . .
would be to let go of "right and wrong"?
That what is "right" for you . . .
is not necessarily so . . .
for me.*

By Your Example

That child who learned . . .
that child in me . . .
learned by your example, Dad . . .
I formed my beliefs
about how men should be.
From the way you lived your life . . .
for the thoughts that you say . . .
and the actions you do . . .
formed the pattern for the way . . .
I should live too.
Yes, Dad, you were the measure . . .
the yard-stick by which
I judged all men.
And by that yard-stick of you . . .
I measured me too.
It's only now that I see it . . .
That the measure was made
from too narrow and short . . .
a stick.

*Oh, Dad . . .
can you not see . . .
that by the narrowness of your mind
you've limited your wisdom . . .
and your ability to love . . .
me?*

Extraordinary People

Extraordinary people . . .
are only ordinary people,
doing extraordinary things.
Stepping out in life . . .
away from . . .
even unpopular
with the crowd.
Like the Eagle . . .
willing to fly higher than the flock.
Being willing to ignore their squawks.
The squawks of Chickens saying . . .
"You can't!"
Telling you what . . .
"You ought."

I Know Your Tears...

My eyes burn with the tears . . .
some shed . . .
some yet to be.
Through a blur I see you . . .
know this ache my heart
is the same in your own.
And my mind goes back
over a quarter century.
I remember the first bloom of our love.
What for others was filthy . . . vulgar . . .
we made clean and pure.
Your tender heart was wounded
together, we healed it by our love.
Where you had only known the lust . . .
the greed . . . the corruption of man,
with me, you found tenderness
and beauty . . .
and honest loving passion.
You responded . . .
gave me your trust.
And for twenty-five years honored me.
You honored me with a son.

Together we nurtured
while he grew into a man.
Then went his own way . . .
as it should be.
Now, alone together . . .
you no longer nurture me,
nor I you.
I have my mountain to climb . . .
Yet, you prefer the comfort
of your gentle valley.
The misty heights
where my heart can soar,
Is not where yours wants to be.
And so we part . . .
and with you will always be
a piece of my heart.
Oh Meg, I know your tears . . .
I hear your cries.
And once again, I ask myself . . .
Why?
Yes . . . why it is I still love you so . . .
Yet in my heart . . .
It's clear . . .
I must go.

An Eagle's Flight—In Poetry

The Battlefield of Unmet Dreams
Chapter 8

The Dream

I am as a man asleep for forty-seven years.
And now . . .
spiritually awakened to a new world.
A world where I am real . . .
emotionally alive . . .
vibrant . . .
But a world where you, my love . . .
are not awake.
Our life together is as a wonderful,
a sweet . . . a loving dream.
Yet I have become an insomniac,
unable . . . unwilling . . . to sleep.
Oh, so much I yearn for the dream.
It draws me . . .
beckons me back to you.
Yet, I cannot sleep again.
That would be death . . .
spiritual death.
And my heart agonizes.
For I know, that soon,
the dream will fade.
And I don't want to be awake . . .
without you.

Inner Quest... The Seminar

IQ . . . the can opener seminar.
Like opening a can of worms,
I opened my heart.
And learned to examine everything
that crawled out.
The three year old hockey-puck . . .
in this game of life.
Slapped around, one relative to the next.
Then abandoned to the orphanage.
To the aloneness . . . the coldness . . .
of uncaring people.
Only filling the physical needs,
uncaring for the unwanted . . .
just doing their job, without love.
Then once again, passed on,
but to another woman.
This surrogate child . . .
A stand in for the one she wanted,
The one she could not have.
IQ . . . the illumination seminar.
Spotlighting these events in my past . . .

And understanding their shadows
in my present.
These beliefs I hold about me,
that keep me prisoner
by the smallness of my mind.
IQ . . . the give-it-up seminar.
Letting go of the story . . .
cutting loose the chains . . .
These comfortable chains,
that bind my life to misery . . .
IQ . . . the seminar for eagles.
Teaching my noble soul to fly.
To soar free above . . .
free of the chains . . .
free of the misery . . .
free to be everything . . .
I care to be!

Surrendering To You

Love . . . love. . .
What have I ever known about love?
Do I love so much
that I make war on you?
Do I love so much
that I hack your tender heart
from your mangled body?
And crush it under my boot,
amongst the gore and rotting relationships
on the battlefield of broken vows.
No!
That I cannot . . .
I will not do!
I surrender . . . belly up . . .
Open to the slash of your sword
that I know will never fall.
I . . . accept . . . you.

To Be...

Inner Quest was a place of safety . . .
A place where I was safe to be
who I wanted to be . . .
to be the person that I was.
Not the one my parents wanted,
taught me to pretend to be . . .
if ever they were to accept me.
I'd painted a mask . . .
colored it with the paint . . .
the paint of their expectations.
I thought to cover the unacceptability . . .
of the real me.
Painted it in skillful pretense,
my performance so intense . . .
I, too, adopted that painted grimace . . .
came to believe it was me indeed.
While inside . . . my heart cried to be free . . .
IQ was a place to see . . .
and learn . . .
learn to just be me.

Flash Floods of Life
Chapter 9

Tigers

The tigers of my mind will come
when I give my ego permission
to hunt . . . to kill.
To bring down another,
to raise my own
self interests.

There is the Tiger of Resentment,
who creeps within . . .
whenever I place
negativity on the event.
For the event, simply . . .
just is.

There is the Tiger of Jealousy,
who creeps within . . .
whenever I blame another . . .
for having what, or being who . . .
I want to be . . .
but know I'm not.

There is the Tiger of Regret,
who creeps within . . .
whenever I wish my life
were other than it is.
When my mind dwells in a past
that never was and now can never be.

There is the Tiger of Condemnation,
who creeps within . . .
whenever I reject
by seeing in others . . .
something I have . . .
and won't look at within me.

There is the Tiger of Revenge,
who creeps within . . .
when I make myself right . . .
by making someone else wrong . . .
to give them the pain I hold within,
in being unacceptable . . . to me.

There is the Tiger of Hate . . .
sister of Revenge,
who creeps within to feed . . .
I send it forth to feed on another . . .
never seeing . . . it only feeds on me.
Like all the tigers of my mind,
'tis me . . . their only sustenance.

What He Heard You Say

Mom, the rage . . .
the bitterness you hold inside . . .
tell me.
For you hold it so well around Dad.
He never saw how you put it away,
out of his sight.
You cared that he not see . . .
But me . . .
With me you could let it show . . .
Let go the bile seething inside.
You could let it flow with me.
But with that . . .
what was the message conveyed to me?
I don't know what that was for you.
I only know what the mind
of that child, who was . . .
relayed to me.
He heard that you loved my Dad.
What he didn't hear . . .
was that you loved . . . me.
I wonder . . .
will he . . .
ever?

Bridges

Every relationship is a bridge . . .
that we build to connect our souls.
Mine may be built of iron and stone . . .
yours of rope and vine.
Yours is the one that takes me to you
Mine brings you to me
Mine will bear the weight of gold
Will yours bear the burden of my ego?
Is it not true that the joy of a gift
is unlimited in the giving?
While my bridge limits not
the gold of your soul,
my ego limits the gifts I can give.
Just as it does, what I can receive.

I Have To Be Right

When what you say or do
makes no sense to me . . .
or I react with negativity,
it can only mean that I am stuck in me.
Stuck in my beliefs . . .
the paradigms of my ego . . .
stuck in, "I have to be right."

For if I could let go of "right" . . .
open my mind to the possibilities,
then I could understand you.
Then, I could see that what works for you,
might also, for me too.

Hanging onto "right"
blinds me . . . deafens me . . .
My "I have to be right," imprisons me.
It keeps me from growing . . .
and it keeps me from knowing . . .
you.

Mirrors

Mom . . . Dad . . .
What was I for you?
In adopting, what was I in your life?
Did I only fill the concept . . .
the meaning . . . the reason . . .
for a good Mormon marriage?
Mother . . . Father . . . Children
a Family.
Could you not have a fulfilling life,
together . . . without?
Was I only there
to make you parents . . .
proud parents?
Just someone to brag about . . .
to complete the show?
Someone to mold
into your own image?
Only loved . . . only accepted . . .
when doing my life as you would . . .
as you taught me?

*Was that my purpose in your life . . .
to be the next you?
Yet . . . isn't a good relationship
really just a bargain . . .
a giving . . . a receiving . . . equally?
Fulfilling one another's needs?
Was it not a paradox . . .
our relationship?
You would only accept me
when I lived as your image . . .
if I carried on your life . . .
after you.
And I?
I wanted someone who would accept . . .
who would love . . .
support me unconditionally.
You weren't . . . you aren't . . .
I wasn't . . . I'm not . . .
Oh, isn't it so sad?
Why not accept one another . . .
support one another
in following our hearts . . .*

*in finding our own dreams . . .
our own joys in life?
To love one another for who we are . . .
not just for what we do?
Of this, you may not agree,
but as for me . . .
I know we are always mirrors . . .
one for another.
And what I see lacking in you . . .
is what needs to be . . . in me.
I need to accept you . . . love you . . .
for just being you.
And I have yet to see
how that will be.*

Have Mercy Baby
Chapter 10
>>> No poetry written for Chapter 11 <<<

Mercy Fuck

I lie here alone
in this big empty bed.
Do you ever think about
the things that I said?
I need some joy, some love,
some meaning in life.
And know I need your help
in ending my strife.
Have mercy, Baby . . .
have mercy on me.
Take this squirt-gun from my hand, Baby,
and set me free.
No one will fault you, Baby . . .
especially not me.
No one will judge,
there will be no jury.
Pull my trigger, Baby,
do a mercy fucking . . .
for me.

Loving, Cheating, and Leaving

A man's acceptance . . .
his love for his mate,
needs not be conditioned
 on her doing anything,
other than being.
Yet still . . . both have needs
that must be met.
And when they are not . . .
I know not how it is with a woman,
only with a man.
Within the whys and wherefores of men . . .
without integrity one loves his mate . . .
and cheats.
With it, one loves her . . .
and leaves.
Seldom do both love enough
to accept such needs and stay.
As seldom do such needs
happen to go both ways.

Mourning

Another day done . . .
and home from work . . .
to an empty house.
I stumble through the mess
scattered about the floor . . .
clean . . . dirty . . .
and in between clothes.
Shower done . . .
I relax here alone
and think of you
and the life we knew,
together.
My eyes flow with tears.
as within my breast,
my heart again breaks.
I allow myself to sob
to wail out in my grief . . .
in my loneliness.
Oh, how long shall it be,
that I'll mourn your death?
Would it be different,
were you not still alive?

Is Love Such a Hard Thing to Swallow
Chapter 12
>>> No poetry was written for Chapter 13 <<<

Sex

With a woman . . .
is sex a glue that bonds,
demands . . . commands . . .
ownership of a man?
To her, is it taking possession?
Is it something given?
Yet in the giving,
expectations of return are made . . .
obligations that must be met.

For a man . . .
perhaps sex is more a conquest,
a challenge,
the red flag in the face of the bull . . .
a glove slapped . . .
a gauntlet flung.
And once conquered,
still free to move on . . .
on to the next challenge.

The glue that bonds him,
demands . . . commands . . .
is when he gives his heart,
not his dick.
Why can't sex just be an experience?
A loving . . . wonderful . . . nurturing . . .
sharing of love.
By two people caring,
one for another.

Reflections

I am responsible for my feelings . . .
my beliefs . . .
my deeds in life.
You . . . for yours.
How you feel about me
is not my concern . . .
only what I feel
and what I see about you.
For it is only the reflection of me . . .
that I see in you.
The words I say . . .
the feelings I feel about you,
tell of the beauty . . .
or of the darkness . . .
in my soul.

Are You The One?

"Are you the one?"
I silently ask of your back.
"The one the fortune teller told me of?
Medium build, medium height,
blonde to reddish hair.
Endowed in a fullness at two points.
You certainly fit the description."
I wait for you to turn.

And then you do.
"No. Pleasant face . . .
even pretty.
Certainly not a beauty, like my Meg."
But then, I look into your eyes.
Bottomless pools of aquamarine . . .
the kind of eyes a man can get lost in . . .
forever.

On an unconscious, unspoken level
we communicate . . .
I feel the pain you hold in your heart.
I know it well.

And I sense the awkwardness . . .
not of grace . . . rather, not feeling wanted.
An uneasiness at being exposed to strangers,
yet, not wanting to be alone.
And silently from my heart,
I send you courage.

Goodbye Letter

It is dark early morn,
alone on my patio,
listening to the freeway
just yards away through the cinder block.
The lights of Las Vegas shine gloriously.
A place that never sleeps.

Sin City . . . Fun Town . . .
I close my eyes and relax.
To Alpha . . .
to the edge of Theta . . .
I summon you,
and to my mind's eye you appear.

Your beauty . . . your grace . . .
the familiar sweet essence of you.
To your higher mind I speak.
I speak of my love for you.
Of all you have meant to me
throughout the years.

And I speak of why,
we can no longer be.

Of my sorrow . . .
and of this agony in my soul.
Then opening my eyes,
I light the match and touch it to the letter.

It takes light and blazes bright . . .
Then fingers scorched,
as the searing of my soul,
I send it off . . .
to the universe . . .
to God . . .
to you.

Doc's Chicken Exit
Chapter 14
>>> No poetry written for Chapter 15 <<<

The Truth About Friends

Doc, my buddy . . .
brother that you were . . .
you taught me of the energy
to meditate . . . intuitively.
You showed me of the psychic power
that each man does possess.
Yet too . . .
you taught me too . . .
of the power of the ego
and how it blinds the truth.
And in the end,
it was the truth about me
as is the truth about every man . . .
that we choose our friends
by the connection we keep,
by the flow of the energy between.
When each man empowers . . .
gives of himself to the other,
the energy of both is more.
But when one wants to take
while the other gives . . .

then the truth about friends
is that the one . . .
and soon both, are gone.
Doc, my friend, my brother . . .
I love you,
but I don't like to be around you.
And I, like the others . . .
am gone.
Still I, like the others . . .
still love you.

Shopping At the Meat Market
Chapter 15
No poetry written for Chapter 15

Eagle Quest
Chapter 16

NOTE OF EXPLANATION:
Eagle Quest was an experiential seminar. On a work detail one lady walked past, her nipples painted lime-green where they imprinted her blouse. Did she do it for me to experience it? Or experience her?

Teressa Nichole Travon

Twin tips colored lime,
draw my eyes and my mind,
to a soul filled with light,
a kindred spirit . . . a delight . . .

On a frame sleek and supple,
to this bachelor means trouble.
In quiet talk she does nourish,
from a heart filled with courage.

On her back I did stand.
Such a heavy demand.
Yet handled the same
as the strength in her name . . .
T. N. T.

ANOTHER NOTE OF EXPLANATION:
As were all the events at Eagle Quest Seminar, they appeared impossible. The lesson with each was that no matter that impossibility in our minds, it is the fear that always stops us. The object was to go until you didn't think you could go any further. Then to take one more step. The failure was to not take that next step past our fear.

One Last Step

The pole . . . the pole . . .
To take that one last step
in balance.
Twice taken . . . Twice failed . . .
And yet . . . twice conquered.
For the win was in the step,
not the outcome.
To repeat a third,
would have been only ego.
As the pole, the fear . . .
was conquered.

Eagle Quest One—The Seminar

We are the ones . . .
The faithful fourteen
for five days
and four nights
we did not quit.
But found the strength within
to go that one more step.
That one step off into flight . . .

No matter the impossibilities,
we did not let our hearts,
our own or other's, down.
And working together,
forged a unit of tempered steel,
our individual weaknesses
supported by the strengths
of the others.

Together there is nothing
we cannot do.
We stand in awe of one another . . .
and love.
With honesty and integrity,
we removed our masks of deceit,

the ones our society hides behind.
Stood naked in the vulnerability
of whom we really are.
And accepted one another . . .
in love.
The quest was to me . . .
personal commitment and support
of more than my share.

Giving up my male ego and privacy . .
in the tent . . .
in the bed . . .
and even in the can.
Honesty and integrity . . .
in every thought, every word,
in every deed.

Challenge of the Soul Mates

Relationships . . .
meeting needs . . . mirroring back . . .
offering each individual soul
the lessons . . . the growth . . .
to complete one's perfection in life.
But Soul Mates?

Soul Mates are as a relationship with wings . . .
uplifted to a higher plane.
Soul Mates exist as an energy combined . . .
immune to gravity . . .
brighter than light . . .
beyond the shades of color . . .

A completeness impossible to one soul alone,
in the honesty of two minds combined.
Our hearts have loved with the tempo of one . . .
Yes, we are Soul Mates . . . you and I.
For I knew this in you, as you knew it in me . . .
once upon a wire.

High up there . . .
My souls burned with a combined fire!
We touched one another with something,
something more intense than even desire.
We fourteen knew it . . .
experienced it, once upon a wire.

There we soared
on the wings of eagles,
knew life as few ever know,
for we have shown to each other
what so few, ever . . .
have the courage to show.

Challenge Eagle

This high wire . . .
This silver band . . .
I carry around my wrist
to remind me of the courage
and the realities about me confessed.
To remind me about the truth of fear,
an illusion, dispelled with every step
I took across the wire.
To remind me that within my soul
resides the passion . . .
the desire . . . the fire.
And to remind me what it is about me,
that I can truly admire.
This high wire . . .
This silver band . . .
Epitomizes all the magnificence,
the who, I truly am . . .
An Eaglet perched upon the wire,
now, one step past my fright . . .
stepping ever into the freedom . . .
and awe . . . of flight.

Single . . . Available . . . Women
Chapter 17

Regina

I greet a friend . . . a buddy . . .
another loving human being . . .
then I see you there.
Tall and slender . . .
a cat-like grace.
I noticed you here before,
just one of several attractive women.
That very attraction, once unapproachable . . .
for me.
Dangerous women . . . risky women . . .
women I might come to love,
commit to . . . be vulnerable to.
Women who might shatter my heart . . .
my icy heart . . . or melt it.
My gaze touches yours . . .
Our eyes lock, and there is a spark.
Like an electrical charge
of silent communication,
and I recognize . . . I remember . . . I know . . .
your very soul.
From somewhere deep within,
I sense . . . I feel . . .
my universe pause,

as if on the brink of an abyss.
A moment of vertigo . . .
then a cord is struck . . .
a heart string plucked . . .
and my soul begins to sing.
I stammer a meaningless question.
Am answered . . . then beat a hasty retreat.
Disorganized . . . confused . . .
unwilling to consider . . .
to believe.
Is it possible you are the one,
the woman of my dreams?
In the seminar I watch from afar . . .
you sit, while those available women stand.
Then when again I approach,
you say you have a man.
Yet your eyes . . .
your beautiful liquid eyes . . .
say "No . . . it is not so."
And in your heart . . .
and mine . . . we know.

Pendulum Swings

The pendulum swings
at the end of its chain . . .
The chain connecting heart to mind.
Channeling . . . communicating . . .
me to me.

"Have I met her yet?" I ask.
— — — — Yes!
I start in surprise,
and feel a flutter deep inside.
I ask again.... and again,
— — — — Yes!

"In the seminar?"
— — — — Yes!
I tick through the women . . .
The ones that make my hormones groan.
— — — — No!
— — — — No!
Then . . .
— — — — Yes!
It is you . . .

And I don't even remember your name.
I'd dismissed you from my mind . . .
unavailable.
Only those eyes . . .
I could not dismiss
those eyes.

Those beautiful . . . those liquid . . .
pools of violet blue . . .
immersible violet blue.
The surface of the pool reflecting,
but not covering . . .
the depths of your soul.

And I remember the spark . . .
that spark . . .
energizing something deep
deep within my own.
Can it be?
Can it really be?
— — — — Yes!

You... So Beautiful You

I sit alone in waiting . . .
sipping coffee . . . anticipating . . .
you.
And what you'll do,
when I present you with
my heart.
Will you ridicule . . .
give it the boot?
Or, hold it gently, lovingly . . .
nurturing everything that we could be . . .
together?
Will you want me as I want you?
Or simply regard me as just another fool,
panting . . . drooling . . .
after you.
I see you arrive . . .
greet you at the door.
I am eager to begin,
trusting the universe . . .
trusting my heart . . .
trusting you.

Oh, so beautiful . . .
you.
We begin to talk . . .
Oh, so little I know
about you.
Most of it says we cannot be,
but my heart says differently.
As you speak, I begin to see
that what my heart says . . .
can really be.
I truly feel . . . I believe . . .
that you are the one . . .
the one for me.
You ask for my poems,
the produce of my heart . . .
A part of me that few have seen.
You ask for them . . .
for all they might mean.
And I see . . . you really do,
want to know me.
The time has come . . .
It is now!

*I hand over my heart in trust . . .
when I give you the poems,
to agree with or disavow.
They speak about love . . .
and of the possibility . . .
it could happen between you and me.
Then breathlessly . . .
I watch you read.
Knowing when you're done,
then, I will know
how you truly feel . . .
Have we won, or come undone.
You read . . . you reread . . .
giving yourself time.
Knowing that if it's "yes" . . .
your life will entwine with mine.
You'll need trust me . . . accept me . . .
while knowing only,
what sets your heart aflame.
I marvel at your courage,
as you simply say . . .
"I feel the same."
YESSS!!!!!*

Move In

Oh Regina, are you a woman of my soul?
Will you join this Eagle's quest?
Perhaps you already have.
The wire of transformation
with its single tethered guide
is it already beneath your feet?.

The green slime in the pits of your life
waits below, to greet you if you fall . . .
Waiting there for those without the courage
to stay the course and cross.
The man to whom you were attached,
no longer provides the support you need.

His rope is played out . . .
Your position is tenuous . . . weakened.
As unstable as is your balance.
Still now, you cling to him
Does he still have the ability
to nurture you?

*Needing more . . . wanting more . . .
you reach out and find me.
Am I the right rope to guide you . . .
lead you . . . support you?
For mine leads in your direction . . .
willingly . . . lovingly . . . with honesty.*

*His does not.
Do you have the strength . . .
the purpose . . . the will . . .
to make the transformation?
Take my rope . . . move with me . . .
move in with me.*

Hard Hearts Sometimes Break
Chapter 18

Righteous

It's all about churches . . .
about being "righteous."
For being "righteous" means being "right."
And being "right" means someone else is "wrong."
And "right" and "wrong" are about war.
And none of it has to be!

Funny thing is . . .
What's "right" may be so
in someone else's mind.
Will I accept it as true in mine?
Is that God's opinion?
I think not!

Why can't my "right"
just mean "right" for me . . .
Your's, "right" for you?
What's true for me,
doesn't have to be . . .
for you.

A church is just a belief system
in someone else's mind . . .
that I adopt . . . in mine,
when I let them tell me what is "right" . . .
and "righteous" . . . for me,
and "wrong" in your church . . . and you.

If either church were truly of God,
would this ever be true?
God's true church is in that part
of my heart . . .
That part telling me what is truth . . .
for me,

That part that is my joy . . .
the same it is within you.
God's church resides within the heart.
It is the Church of Love.
Love and God are the same . . .
everywhere.

Judging You

Forgive me, Mom, for judging you . . .
for thinking I needed to forgive.
You are you . . .
And I know you love me
in the way that you were taught.
It is the best way you know how.
I thank you, Mom, for loving me . . .
and for doing it . . . your way.
For had you not,
I would not know this.
Nor would I know . . . or be . . .
who I am, right now!

Mom... Dad

The rift between us . . .
the abyss . . .
is so deep and far across.
Is it your hardness of hearing
or the hardness of your heart,
that keeps you deaf
to me?

Or is it just
that the distance between
has become so great?
My paradigms of thinking have changed.
And like a different current,
perhaps higher in my mind,
they carry me away from you.

It is not possible . . .
not even within my power . . .
to go back.
You ask me to be responsible . . .
to live my life in misery.

*Chained to a woman,
when I can never again be
who she wants me to be.*

*I will not be
unfaithful to me.
I must follow my heart.
You ask me to accept guilt . . .
take responsibility . . .
for your anger.
To make you right . . .
for hating me.*

*Is it really I
who is selfish?
Being unwilling to live in misery . . .
so that you need not choose
to hate . . .
to be angry . . .
disappointed . . .
in me.*

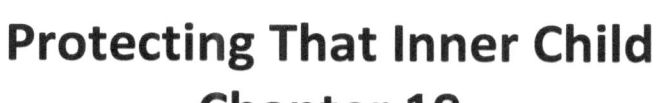

Protecting That Inner Child
Chapter 19

Heirloom

I feel the rage burning deep inside,
at something my child has done.
Out of my mouth it bursts . . .
demeaning him . . .
telling him how little he's worth.
These years later, I look inside me,
and see . . .
it was really all about me.

Merely something that he'd done,
that pulled the trigger of my gun.
Pulling it with a finger from my own past.
Back then, when I too . . .
learned "worthless."
Oh, how I hope that it won't be
the same with his child
and he.

For I've talked with him . . .
told him from my heart . . .
what it's really all about.
Still . . .
I know that he,
like me . . .
now carries the same trigger . . .
on the same gun.

My hope is that he
is much wiser
than me,
wise enough to see . . .
it is only an old family heirloom . . .
worthless . . .
much less . . .
than love.

New Mommy

I have a new Mommy.
Joyously . . . jubilantly, I pulled at your hand . . .
dragging you . . . showing you around.
To the orphans I knew
in that dispassionate place . . .
a place I have now escaped.
The song of my joy,
I sang it loud . . .
proclaiming my joyous triumph.
I have a new mommy . . .
and she will love and care . . . for me!
Unlike my brother, I accepted you....
welcomed you with open heart.
And unlike him, didn't consciously see....
that was only so . . . for me.
Yes, I accepted you in love.
You were ". . . my new mommy!"
I did not see you never accepted me.
I was never ". . . your new son."
Rather, only a substitute . . .
like a rubber doll,
for that one you could never have.
For that one you would accept . . . with love.

Of Shoelaces, Trust, & Self Esteem

I look down the blue of my corduroyed legs
to the free flung laces of my shoes.
It is because of me, that they swing so free.
Yes, they flap with delight,
a comforting sight,
for I have a new mommy,
and she will tie them . . . just for me.

My heart is as light
as my four year old feet,
skipping gaily into your room.
With joy and elation, I pull-off my ruse,
"Mommy, Mommy, come tie my shoes!"
Your anger and disgust wither my smile,
as into my face you unload.

"How many more times must I show you?"
Kneeling on the floor, just as before,
again you do the ritual.
"This over that, you loop this,
you loop that, over and under,
now you're done."

Then loosed with a flick, "Now YOU do it!"
Idly I toy with it, my heart not here,
on something I need not know,
You are my new mommy;
you will take care of me now . . .
I know.

Smiling shyly, I look up . . .
Look into your eyes,
your eyes of rage . . . bulging . . .
distended with the furor of your emotions.
I'm shocked at your unexpected fit,
and the spite in your eyes as the words hit.

"Whatever possessed me,
to take on such a stupid little shit?
I should have had my head examined!"
From the closet, my suitcase,
thrown down before the dresser,
my single drawer, jerked open.

All possessions of mine,
all the worth of me.
"Get your things . . . get out!"

Through the blur of tears,
I pack my clothes.
Then out into the hall I shuffle.

My stuffed red horse,
only friend . . . loyal companion,
tucked safely under my arm.
Together we feel the whoosh . . .
hear the slam of the door,
behind us . . .

The hallway dark . . . old and cold,
of an apartment house
built early in the century.
With the promise of the mines . . .
the boom of Bingham Canyon . . .
like me now, somehow sadly, left behind.

Suitcase at the door, reaching, struggling,
both hands turning the brass knob.
Its touch as frigid as this chill in my heart,
like the ice crystalled glass,
encrusting the pane in the heart
of the door's long center part.

Outside the air is biting,
the sun, a dim disc in a coal smoke smudge,
breathed in,
a grunge on every frosted breath.
At the bottom porch step we stop.
Huddled together,
my frayed friend and me,
I hug him tight,
to stop him of his shivering.

Staring down the narrow walkway
of snow banks cresting overhead . . .
Cold, oh so cold . . .
the chill stabs at my nose
pulls tight the ice choked hairs inside.
How will we stay warm? Where will we go?
Is there a warm place somewhere to hide?

Eternity passes . . . then you come for us.
Taking us back inside,
to the warmth of your home . . .
and the coldness . . . of your icicle heart.
Tears you cry, and say you love me . . .
say you're sorry . . .
yet, I question every part.

Are the tears really for me?
Are you really sorry?
Can I ever believe your heart?
Are your words your decoy,
when you tell me
I'm a good little boy.

And though you say it,
how will it truly go?
You say you'll always take care of me.
Yet, I know . . . in my heart, I know . . .
that I'm not good enough . . . for you,
and you won't be there . . . for me.

Will it always be,
that the women I love will see . . .
what you now, have taught to me?
Will my love . . .
ever . . .
be "good enough?"

An Eagle's Flight—In Poetry

Thirty Days, Babe
Chapter 20

Eagle Quest Two

Here at EQ Two . . .
supporting . . . on staff . . .
being of service to others.
Growing . . .
as I help them to grow.
Supporting new Eaglets
as they climb the pole.
They finish . . . the last is done.
Thrilled . . . exuberant . . .
in awesome wonder of themselves.
Each one going further
than ever they thought they could.
Each one basking in the glow . . .
in the magnificence of their soul.
Now the question is raised . . .
Will I go next?
I feel my nerves tighten . . .
a tinge of fear . . . and more.
Resentment . . .
for feeling there is no choice.

*I must back my words . . .
my encouragement to them . . .
with action.
The resentment,
I see as a choice for me.
Coupled with fear . . .
it can mean one thing . . .
opportunity.
I feel the fear gather
as I climb the pole.
I ask myself why?
Twice I've climbed . . .
and twice at the top,
taken that one last step....
That one step I'd feared
I would not take.
Yet it is not a fear,
not even a concern
that I will not this time.
So why this fear
that troubles me so?
This nameless dragon
of my mind.*

To what about it, am I blind?
What won't I see, about me?
As I crest the top,
my eyes peer over
eight inches of flat wooden circle . . .
at the trapeze beyond.
It is now I see . . .
it is now I know my fear.
Twice I have fallen from this perch,
never reaching the bar, the goal.
Satisfied in having done my best
in taking that one last step....
That one step past my fear.
Both times before you were on that bar,
my goal . . . my woman . . . my mate.
I wanted you then,
yet you had no face,
no body . . . no name . . . no grace.
I only knew of your soul,
of the essence within you . . .
who now has a name . . . Regina.
I can not fail!

*I will not fail . . .
of failure is my fear.
I am at the top,
just one more step . . .
The pole is swaying . . .
my legs are shaking . . .
I feel weakness to the bone.
I take some time
to center my mind . . .
to do it differently
this time.
I gather my strength . . .
feel my resolve . . .
one more quick step, then I leap.
My body arcs.... I catch the bar!
The triumph, my love,
is sweet.*

Broken Promises and Lies

Thirty days have come and gone,
unnoticed . . . unmarked . . . by you.
Instead of wearing this horned dog to a stub,
you kissed him on the cheek
as you sailed off to your gym.
I want to be closer
than the sheen on your skin-tight blue jeans,
to nestle with you in the gap of your thighs
where we can glorify our love.
Yet, I just feel alone . . . so alone.
Familiar patterns . . .
Up till three, avoiding that bed.
That bed where I sleep alone . . .
Alone, with you by my side . . .
unapproachable . . . unlovable . . .
unavailable and alone.
I lie beside you and am so conscious of my
promise . . .
The promise of space . . .
to bother you no more with my conversation
or my touch.
The promise binding me from expressing my love,
leaves only tears to fill my heart.

Yet, especially in this,
I am bound to silence.
For it would only drag you down . . .
with my grief . . . my depression.
I place no blame of it on you.
Yet soul mates uplift one another . . .
support in times of need.
Am I just too needy?
I don't want to be.
I lie here beside you . . .
watching you snoring softly,
oblivious to me.
I gently touch your thigh,
lying to myself . . .
saying the promise is only broken
should you wake.
Quietly, I whisper
the contents of my heart.
Perhaps my whisper
carries too much feeling,
for you feel it . . .
and half-awake, mumble,
"Are you talking to me?"

"No," I lie.
It is number one.
The lie I swore I would never tell.
Then, quickly caught, I tell the truth.
"Yes."
Yet, before I blink, comes number two . . .
"It's okay . . . go back to sleep."
Oh, Regina . . .
I feel our love dying,
like a captured animal,
bleeding to death . . . in agony.
Caught by the steel jaws
of this trap called promise.
The promise of space . . .
A promise that herein, I break,
with a request for my hearts sake.
Is it really the space you need to take?
Or perhaps . . .
a decision you need to make?
The space you request closes intimately,
or widens infinitely.

Carpe Diem

"Good things come to those who wait."
It is a lie!
Death comes to those who wait.
Even in their living are they dead.

Carpe diem!
Capture the day!
Because the night will always fall
when you are not looking.
I know my mortality . . .
For I've looked into Death's unblinking eye.
Felt his chill fingers within my breast . . .

And know that someday soon . . . too soon,
I will come to be just dust and bone,
Tumbling . . .
floating on the winds of time,
down home again . . .
One with, once more, those shady canyons,
the ancient homeland of the Anasazi.

*Yet, beside you last night . . .
giving you time . . . giving you space . . .
I felt myself stirring.
With a need . . . a want,
both from within my heart,
and within my shorts.*

*So much love and comfort,
we could be sharing . . .
yet, are not.
Someday, too soon, it will be
as a widow's tears on the dust and bone.
And dusty bones make such a poor lover.*

*Carpe diem!
Capture the day!
For it is the first, or last . . .
of the rest of our lives,
my love.*

Shark Bite

Soul mates . . . matching souls . . .
Yes . . . perhaps in another life.
The conscious personalities
now have different bends.
Not accepting of him,
you saw freedom in me.
Only to be stifled by my love . . .
or was it my need?
An impossibility for my soul mate.
Where I only wanted to be close . . .
to talk . . . to touch . . .
you wanted solitude . . .
to read . . . to meditate.
And my heart,
my guarded heart,
did not feel safe with you . . .
to just be me.
For in my heart I knew,
only time would bring your judgment
and the axe would fall.
As with him . . . so with me.
Now you return to him.

You say for a completion.
But what of me . . . of us?
Are you complete with me?
Did you only use my love as the axe
to cut him down . . .
shape him like a totem?
Will you ever see
neither he nor I will ever be
who you want?
Because you are not who you want?
Other people are mirrors for us.
If I can see it in them,
it is always in me.
Yet, I did not see your use of me.
Perhaps it's no longer in me to see.
Of all the fish in the sea,
your soul was a match for me.
Here to teach these lessons of life,
necessary for me to be
all that I can be.
There are sharks in the waters,
beautiful . . . graceful . . . sometimes deadly.
I look in the mirror . . .
am I one still?

Burying the Past
Chapter 21

Sir Knight

Your Sir Knight is dead.
Pierced through . . .
Impaled on a shaft
from the light of consciousness.
No longer to ride to your rescue.
To slay the dragons of your mind,
and rescue you from your emotions.
Yes, your Sir Knight has fallen.
Taking down with him your shield of security.
And your sword of power . . . of control.
The drama is done.
With what now will I replace him,
and give you security from your fears?
Money?—I have none.
Social position?—It's an illusion.
Power?—You already possess all you need.
Wisdom?—Again . . . also within you.
I will replace him with that
which I give you freely.
I will replace him with love . . .
Unconditional love.

Do Eagles Always Soar Alone?

I see the anguish in your eyes,
and with tears streaking my face,
as the blood
from these wounds in my soul,
voice quavering, I say the words . . .
"It is over."
I love you, yet,
I no longer fill your need
for domination and control . . .
the security in your life
the foundation . . .
for our marriage.
Once your submissive husband-child,
I've grown up . . . found courage . . .
Courage to step out to the edge . . .
to try my wings . . .
and soar.
Your fears will not let you nurture
or join me in my quest . . .

It is over . . .
and my quest goes on.
Alone I sit at this table,
where once we ate,
laughed, and loved.
It now holds only loneliness,
feathers ruffled . . .
mildewed from my tears.
It is cold in these rarefied heights,
and oh, so solitary . . .
Do eagles always . . .
soar alone?

Farewell, My Love

My heart is elsewhere . . .
suspended between time . . .
between space.
No tangible existence.
Tied to you it cannot move on.
Our marriage . . .
our dance of life . . .
is finished.
Yet, my heart won't let go.
It is bound to yours
by the glue of love
and twenty-five years . . .
enraptured.
I must not linger . . .
Our dance is over.
And now somewhere waits . . .
a new partner.

One who wants me.
To the end of alpha . . .
the dawn of theta, I go.
I must take up the sword,
endure the agony,
of slicing my heart loose . . .
from yours.
Farewell my love . . .
Oh God give me strength!
Farewell . . .

Dawn

These arms of mine once held the sky . . .
embracing love as few men know.
Then darkness came and we lost the flames
we shared within our souls.
One went off to school,
in another, the passion cooled . . .
Of the rest we had little common fuel.

Yes, our fires had dimmed . . .
And Death found me then,
no longer aflame . . .
Just one . . .
of two bitter victims.
Now its memory exists
ghostly hot within my breast.

Through the dark of night,
ghostly memories smolder
in lonely fright . . .
tis time they too,
must die.
For it's only in one's night
can there come such light.

In the break of this new dawn,
night can escape . . . dissipate . . .
expand and change . . .
as it moves on.
Leaving room . . .
making space . . .
for a new love to grow upon.

Does your heart, too,
feel this yearning . . .
for a new love
bright and burning . . .
as the new light
of this . . .
new dawn?

Motorcycle Wheels and Macho Balls
Chapter 22

Sparring With the Dinosaur

Twelve years I rode the 350XL,
Honda's trusty little Enduro.
Made for on or off the road.
I preferred the back country,
dirt mountain roads . . .
sand swept trails . . .
Colorado's mountains . . .
Utah's canyon lands.
I loved it so.
Yet, the highway . . . the blacktop . . .
held a fear for me.
In competition with the gleaming hulks . . .
like sparring with the dinosaur.
Fragile . . . puny . . .
no match for them.
To be be squashed . . .
just another bug smear,
spread across a bumper.
I parted with my XL . . .
old friend . . . trusty companion . . .
moved to the city.

To Las Vegas . . . tinsel town . . .
A blacktop jungle full of crazies,
drunks, and druggies . . .
A deadly asphalt . . . battlefield.
Five years I cowered to the fear.
Longing ever for the wind . . .
magic wind against my face.
Flying free beneath the slick-rock cliffs
and mountains that I loved so.
And for the power . . .
throbbing . . . purring . . .
surging between my thighs.
Then came the day I thought my last.
When I labored weakly,
struggling for breath . . .
just a few more moments of life in sight.
Knowing . . . seeing . . .
dreading the end.
In the mirror of Death, I looked at life . . .
and mourned the wasted hours . . .

The hours spent in fear . . .
only added to the years . . .
the years I spent in dying.
That day, I thought my last, was truly . . .
my wake up call to courage.
The courage I saw within my soul . . .
and welcomed within my life . . .
should any more life be known.
These days I ride another ride
better suited for the jungle.
A machine of ball busting,
gut wrenching, rumbling fury . . .
my Virago 1100.
Arriving home, I set the stand . . .
fresh off that asphalt battlefield.
And feel the thrill . . .
the chill tingle of adrenalin . . .
coursing sprightly with my blood . . .
and I know . . . I am . . . alive!
I have sparred once more
with the dinosaur . . .
and won.

*Today has been just for one more day,
that I have lived in truth . . .
A truth once seen in the face of Death,
once smelled upon his breath.
If I spend my life giving way to fear,
not doing because of the danger . . .
then I . . . am not . . . alive.
This life is full of danger . . .
our fear begs we run from Death,
when in truth, we run only from life.
Far better to recognize danger . . .
respect it . . . be aware . . .
even occasionally give it berth.
Yet never . . . give it fear.
And in the end, when death does come . . .
I will know . . . that I . . .
have lived.*

Fears

Make friends with your fears,
for they are the dragons of your growth.
Never fly them high
on the winds of your paranoia,
or they will become the masters of your life.
Rather, bridle them with loving control . . .
open-minded understanding . . .
and they will serve you faithfully,
pointing out the things about you . . .
the ones you most need to see.
Yes . . . make friends with your fears
and they will respond
and make you wonderful . . .
loving pets.

The Snuggle

I feel your spirit . . . your presence . . .
the energy of your being.
It kindles a matching flame in my heart,
as you crawl into my lap and snuggle.
The way your body fits mine . . .
as if putting on an old familiar
and loved pair of soft leather gloves.
You feel so natural . . .
an extension of me.
As my hand lightly strokes
your lithe firm body,
I feel your energy
as a sense of well-being.
A warm glow
I haven't felt since the age of four,
with my only friend and companion . . .
a stuffed red horse.
And my whole world pauses,
peaceful, in contentment.

Passions

We parted . . .
after twenty-five years of marriage.
I still loved you,
yet would no longer subjugate myself . . .
my power . . . to you.
I left . . .
pulled up the thread of my life.
Went on without you,
and came to know others.
Yet found my passion . . .
My need . . .
showed as only a shadow . . .
a facsimile . . .
of what we had together.
I met a woman of beauty . . .
of passion . . . and magnificence.
And wanted to know her . . .
and to love her with all the passion
in my heart.
I found myself artful,
but still only a shadow . . .

An artful shadow
of the man I wanted to be . . .
of one I know I am.
Then one night we quarreled.
And later, in bed, she said.
"Not tonight. I'm not in the mood."
Yet, there was a fire . . . a passion . . .
I stroked her . . . touched her . . .
thought I felt her respond.
And I took her with all the fire . . .
the thunder of a rocket launch.
While she merely allowed . . .
yet, mid flight . . . I saw
she only watched the fireworks,
but lit no rockets of her own.
In shock . . . and disgust of my insensitivity,
I stopped.
Yet she urged me on . . .
said she would ride this rocket to the end,
to the star-burst of my desire.
And she did.
I've thought long . . . and hard . . .
and deeply.

*I've looked within . . . and without . . .
and struggled about . . .
until I could see the truth of it in me . . .
this truth that sickens and disgusts me.
My God . . .
Am I Pavlov's dog?
Conditioned with years
to respond to the challenge,
but only the challenge . . .
of igniting the passions
in a cold unresponsive woman.
This game I will not accept,
being played between me and my mate.
My passion was only the sick response . . .
My rock-hard cock, my offered part
In my attempt to bribe . . . a controlling . . .
unloving heart?*

Perceptions

Hurt feelings . . .
Misconceptions . . .
Understandings not connected . . .
In a moment of vulnerability,
a rejection only perceived
still hurts the same.
Honest communications . . .
the only medicine to cure a wounded soul.
Those self-inflicted wounds . . .
cut deeply by unreal realities.
A kiss spurned in a crowded room.
Are you ashamed of me? . . .
Am I beneath you? . . .
Not acceptable to your friends? . . .
Or are you only saving . . .
sparing the sensitivities of another?
Unwilling to face their drama.
A former lover . . . a rival discarded . . .
rejected in reality.
Yet, where would I go?

Away . . . alone . . .
avoiding you . . .
Have I not the courage to face you . . . to clarify?
What am I so afraid of, that again,
I would play these silly games?
Games beneath my noble soul.
Would I begrime the purity of me?
Even were my original perception
to be in perfect sync with yours,
Could I not still accept your weakness?
It's a lonely perch for me,
if the ones you love,
always sit below you.
Yes perhaps I could . . .
Perhaps I'll circle a time and see,
if there's any room on your perch
for me.

Judgment

I wear what I wear . . .
I like it.
Why do you care?
Do you judge me?
Am I a nerd in your mind?
Yet in the true reality of life,
we only judge ourselves . . .
not others.
What is not acceptable of me . . .
to you,
is in truth, not acceptable for you . . .
to you.
My clothes on you,
might make you a nerd . . .
to you.
My clothes on me,
just satisfy my needs.
For me . . .
they simply cover my butt.

An Eagle's Flight—In Poetry

Ka-Bar
Chapter 23

Memorial Day

Two abreast . . . Old Glory streaming . . .
Rumbling . . . thundering . . .
Reverberating off the canyon walls.
Pulsating the air . . .
Shivering the very concrete
of the dam.
Hoover Dam . . .
holding back the mighty Colorado.
Leading off the pack . . .
the unsung heroes in parade,
paying tribute to their long lost brothers,
who died at Charlie's hand.
The Vietnam Vets Motorcycle Club,
proudly flying their colors,
and Old Glory.
Followed up by 120 misfit Harleys . . .
and one lone rice burner.
A salute of honor, long past due . . .
Parading the dam in thundering,
rumbling glory . . .
Answered with the crowd's applause.
A memorial to the brave . . .
the missing . . .
those who bled . . .
and the dead.

Sometimes Life Changes And Remains the Same
Chapter 24

Burger Barn

Lunch at Burger Barn . . .
Gazing out the window
at distant mountains beckoning . . .
A swish of movement,
a whiff of delicate perfume . . .
distracts me.

I look up at the slim figure
gracefully gliding by.
Long hair flowing black . . .
perfect figure . . .
She turns as she sits,
eyes meeting mine . . .

Dark reddish brown . . .
widely spaced . . . almond shaped . . .
exotically beautiful oriental eyes.
Her face delicately featured . . .
exquisitely lovely . . .
like my Meg.

Then through my mind flashes
twenty five years of loving her . . .
even still.
Deliberately . . .
my eyes return to the mountains . . .
distant mountains . . .

That distance suddenly heavy on my mind.
Stretching . . .
vastly away . . .
Like the rest of my life . . .
without her.
Such a vast lonely stretch.

As always . . . I ground myself,
connect to Mother Earth.
Feel my butt, pressed into the chair
see the fan overhead,
gently stirring the air . . .
feel the air as it kisses my skin.

I smell the aroma,
char-broiled burgers and fries . . .
breathed in on every breath.
Now grounded,
back here to the present . . .
away from the past and future . . .

The pain is gone in the here . . .
in the now.
I'm aware of the people . . .
where they are all around . . .
Especially all those other women,
in this luncheon crowd.

Those beautiful ones . . .
those ugly ones . . .
as my perception dictates.
All, could be there in the hours . . .
the days . . . the years . . .
stretching before me.

Friends, even lovers . . .
sharing their lives with mine . . .
giving . . . receiving . . . together.
If I am alone in this world,
it is only by choice.
My choice . . .

Forgive Me My Love

Oh, so long it has been,
since last I saw you Dear.
Near a year since we parted . . .
The love I held for you still swells
within my heart.
Your beauty, still,
a comfort to my gaze
across this restaurant table.
Oh, so much has happened
in my life.
So much growth to my soul . . .
And so much,
I want to hear of yours.
Yet, you are silent . . .
strangely silent.
I ask with gentle prodding . . .
open ended sentences . . .
Still, so little will you say.
Then, with a start,
the answer crystallizes . . .
clearly now . . .
obvious to my mind.

Your life hasn't changed . . .
You, haven't changed . . .
It is only I, who has.
You still live that life
of quiet desperation.
Seeking only comfort . . .
seeking security . . .
where none exists . . .
nor ever will.
Walking down that path
of living death . . .
asleep to the ecstasy
that could be yours,
should you awaken
the freedom of your spirit . . .
the wisdom of your soul.
My heart bleeds
great tears of sorrow . . .
For I see how lonely
your own must be . . .
I feel it from your energy.
You walk your path alone . . .
no company.

Alone with only your memories . . .
No longer to walk it with me.
Forgive me, my love,
for not staying . . .
An enlightened soul not growing . . .
is dying.
Were it only this body, for you,
a thousand deaths
I would gladly suffer.
Yet, with my soul . . .
not even one.
Forgive me, my love . . . forgive me.
For my mind tells me I am wrong . . .
for what my heart tells me is right.
And to my soul,
I feel the agony . . .
for I know that what is,
must be . . .
And what was,
is gone . . .
forever.

Painting Pink Turds
Chapter 25

Leasha

The death knell of our relationship
was the sound of sorrow . . .
My grieving for a loved one
now in my past.
I told you, Leasha, of my pain . . .
shared with you my sorrow.
Yet, what you heard,
that panicked you into the night was
"I'm not available . . . to you."
Those weren't the words, yet . . .
I don't know . . . perhaps that was so.
Doubly so . . . now.
Goodbye, Leasha, my best friend . . . lover . . .
Again I feel the pain . . . the sorrow.
I don't know where we were going . . .
we never got there.
Thank you for this lesson . . .
'Twill never be the same . . .
ever.
Yes, Leasha . . .
I created this relationship
even to the drama of your leaving.

*By not being there as you wanted,
in love-struck, moon-eyed drooling.
Searching out . . . doing . . .
what pleases you.
Trying to "make you happy."
Perhaps it is just my way
of searching . . . weeding . . .
for the one who stays . . .
for the one who won't leave.
For that one
who finds unimaginable happiness
in being here with me,
here only because she wants to be.
That, is the woman . . .
with whom I want to be.*

An Eagle's Flight—In Poetry

Riding a Bad-Assed Machine
Chapter 26

In the Wind

Sometimes in the wind . . .
in the numbing coldness . . .
or the warming heat of it,
I feel . . . I know . . .
life!
Right here . . . right now . . .
life!
Living in the present,
and the ever presence of Death.
Yet, living . . .
For we are all . . .
always . . .
in the ever presence of Death . . .
though not all are living
in the presence of life.
Sometimes passing the semi . . .
inches away . . .
the spinning, rumbling wheels of death.
The wind in my face at eighty . . .
gusting . . . twenty . . .
thirty more.

The expectation of the wake
at the semi's face . . .
knowing . . .
the jarring force of it to come.
Will it throw me . . .
slam me down . . .
down to the cold hard ground?
Suck me under those giant wheels . . .
rushing . . .
churning ever around?
Or will it merely buffet . . .
wildly once . . .
then gone . . .
as through the wind, I rush on.
Living ever . . .
in the ever presence . . .
of life . . .
of Death . . .
here . . .
now!

Sedona

I drop from the rim.
Following the two lane,
switching back and forth . . . steeply,
turning sometimes, on itself.
I feel the power surging beneath,
responding flawlessly to my control.

I hear the deep burble,
and occasional popping backfire,
of my exhaust.
It is almost as a salute . . .
a greeting, one power to another.
For I also feel the power . . .
the presence of Oak Creek Canyon.

A majestic . . . stately . . .
almost solid presence . . .
acknowledged from deep within.
Then the canyon opens up . . .
sandstone cliffs and monoliths,
stand in grandeur, all around.

*Marred only by the buildings . . .
the assumed ownership of mankind,
owned only in the ego of his mind.
In the middle of it all,
the town . . .
Sedona.*

*Rows of quaint shops.
A forced quaintness . . . artificial.
I park my bike.
Still slightly numb . . .
dazed from the buffeting
of 350 miles of wind.*

*A part of me is eager to see . . .
to explore the shops.
Another part angry.
Like Jesus in the temple,
I wish to drive out this greed . . .
rub clean, this mar to perfection.*

For a while I wander.
Then, getting late, I ask of a place to camp.
In my mind . . . showers . . . amenities . . .
Indignantly, I am told,
"You can't just camp . . .
You must use a camp park!"

Am I a scourge, a louse upon this land . . .
and cannot be left free?
Free to be where Sedona wants me to be.
I motor west on 89A.
Then turning south, I find a trail . . .
off into the trees . . . beneath a rim.

A private spot . . .
hidden away.
I set up my camp and grab a snack . . .
then find a special spot.
By the side of a wash, beneath a cedar,
I sit upon a rock.

Counting down I relax . . .
edging Alpha to Theta . . .
grounding myself to the Earth.
I feel the energy . . .
the flowing of it through me.
And I ask the question . . .

"Why Sedona . . .
Why did you call me?"
The answer comes
from deep within . . .
as a feeling, it says . . .
"To heal . . . It is time to heal!"

I think of the sore upon my leg . . .
stinking . . . burning . . . oozing . . .
sometimes screaming out in pain.
A symptom, the outward sign
of the one upon my heart . . .
the one I am here to heal.

A Cry in The Silence

The rock is solid beneath my butt,
yet, warmed from the sun above.
I wonder where I will get the strength
to warm this stone cold heart . . .
where once resided my love.
My body relaxes within itself,
hands rested upon my thighs,
in through my nose I inhale my breath.
Up from the earth . . . down from above . . .
I fill with the energy of creation's love.
Then out through my mouth
I exhale the sorrow . . .
the pain . . . the grief long held.
Out it comes . . . a high . . . a reedy wail . . .
the anguish of my soul.
Washed along . . . away with the tears.
Away Meg . . . I wash you away.
No longer do I hold you to me.
No longer will I allow this wound . . .
this wound that festers,
a poison to my soul.

Lessons, Tests, & Validations
Chapter 27

The Correction

Index fingers pointed inwardly . . .
accusingly . . .
I say the words of truth . . .
of change . . .
"The correction—*always*—goes here."
I cannot change you . . .
who you are . . .
what you do . . .
I can only change me.
Change my mind . . .
my viewpoint . . .
the paradigms of my thinking,
and thus, how I feel
and what I do.
You are not what you do.
It is not what you do
that makes you unacceptable.
Rather, how I feel about it.
And that, I can choose to change,
if I want to accept you . . .

Loving Lucy

Yes, I loved Lucy . . .
Saw it all there in her to see . . .
and accepted it as her right to be.
With her, I offered the gift of me,
and then moved on.
Perhaps sometime she too, will see . . .
just what it was for her to see,
in the mirror of me.

Best Friends

She was my best friend . . .
sometimes lover . . .
Someone to explore life with.
With her, I felt loved . . .
respected . . . safe.
With her, I felt accepted.
Until one night, we two alone,
I spoke a chance remark
full of jovial . . . sexual . . .
fun-poking innuendo.
She went to anger . . .
hurt . . .
perceived disrespect,
and set up a boundary . . .
a wall . . .
a distance between . . .
across our fields of love.
"You can't talk that way to me!
I am a lady . . .
I won't allow it!"

She threw out the eggshells
of her feelings,
"Don't you dare . . .
don't you ever . . .
step on them!"
Now the fields
have lost their flowers.
I don't see them . . .
while looking for . . .
avoiding, those shells.
And my heart
now mourns my friend . . .
once, sometimes lover.
Now buried somewhere . . .
somehow . . .
sadly beneath them.
Alongside the loving safety . . .
we two . . .
once knew.

Once in the Eclipse of a Blue Moon
Chapter 28

Eclipse of the Blue Moon

Las Vegas . . .
up before light and on the bike . . .
traveling throughout the day.
Stopping only for burgers . . . gas . . .
and to empty my ass . . .
'till dusk finds me pitching tent.
Darkness descending along with the chill . . .
back full-circle to where our lives
played out together . . .
growing apart,
back once more . . .
to Farmington.
Pitching tent by the light
of a blue full moon . . .
Yet not . . .
for it is shadowing over . . .
bit by tiny bit . . .
in a total eclipse.
Like our life together . . .
our love . . .
slowly dying . . .
consumed . . .

*Like a dream that wasn't real . . .
or real needs that were never met.
Sitting at this KOA upon a picnic table,
I watch it unfold again . . .
And shiver in the bitter cold
as bit by tiny bit . . .
the moon's pearly glow . . .
the life we knew . . .
is turned to a dim dark globe . . .
a dull and dirty burnt orange marble.
Lingering for a time in malevolent glow
that slowly fades near black.
Yes, I watch it all just so,
and shiver in the bitter cold.
The bitter cold . . .
like my life this day . . .
its warmth just ebbing away . . .
The dreams . . . the love . . .
the material things . . .
all gone . . . all finished . . .
slipped from my grasp . . .
a shattered crystal vase.
Nothing left but the icy
cold twinkling*

Shards of a million tiny frosted stars,
and the cheery flashing of a passing plane:
A friend signaling . . .
telling me that life is not gone . . .
not all lost.
That soon a new moon will be uncovered.
New life . . . new love . . .
I may use this time to clear my mind . . .
and straighten out my life . . .
in making room anew . . .
for a new loves pearly glow.
Yes, how often will the eclipse . . .
the old love . . . old life end?
For me, it happens only once . . .
once in the eclipse of a blue moon.

Thurs. Sept 26th, 1996

The Ghost of Durango Calling Me
Chapter 29

And My Memory of You . . .

Yes, I left you my love,
took a different path . . .
away . . . alone.
'Though simply within,
it still carries me apart . . .
away where you fear to go.
Yet still . . . my memory of you . . .
Is love.

I still carry within my heart,
the loving memories,
inscribed upon my soul . . .
of what we used to do,
and how it used to be.
Me holding you . . . you holding me.
For my memory of you . . .
Is love.

I remember the walks along the hills,
among the Buddhist shrines . . .
In the cool of a Korean summer's morn.
Your slender body a flowing grace . . .
within your red silk gown,
with the zipper down the front.

And my memory of you . . .
Is love.

And I remember the nights . . .
frosty Korean winter's nights.
Snuggled warm beneath the spread . . .
our arms . . . our legs . . .
our bodies entwined.
And my memory of you . . .
Is love.

Later . . . our life,
our marriage together,
and the son you bore.
Your gift to me . . .
your gift to the world . . .
Paid for with shrieks
and agonized wracking spasms,
delivering your love
from within your womb.
And my memory of you . . .
Is love.

And I remember your loving
nurturing hands,
as together we raised him . . .

tall and sure.
Together we built our home,
upon the sage
and wild-flowered meadows,
pinion pine and cedar forests,
of our Rocky Mountain land.
Yes, together we built it all,
just "ekjackly" so.
And my memory of you . . .
Is love.

When in the end, came time to die
I recognized the lie.
Our life together was as I describe . . .
It was my reality . . . for me,
'though never yours . . . for you.
Was my reality the lie you told you?
Was that why you would never look too,
never look within you . . .
not for what was right or wrong,
but merely for the truth?
Still, my memory of you . . .
Is love.

For me . . .
I've traveled the path . . .
moved past the pain . . .
 the sad "if onlys" of then.
My memories of the life we shared
carry only the wonder of love.
Something I hold,
a pleasure always . . .
here within my heart.
Because my memory of you . . .
Is love.

Annyonghi kesipsiyo,
chaemi manhi pogo kapnida.
These words you taught me
to say to others . . .
never realizing I'd say them now.
Goodbye, my love,
I had a wonderful time.
And know in your heart . . .
that my memories of you . . .
will always be . . .
of love.

What Was It Calling Me?

Farmington . . . seven years gone . . .
And Sis, the office girl,
is the only one remembers . . .
the only one to recognize me.
Even old friends only see . . .
me, a Harley freak . . .
on my Yamaha Virago.
Why am I here?
What was it . . . calling me?

Then, on to Durango . . .
over ten years past . . .
and a misty eyed view . . .
the land we once knew,
and the house we built.
Seeing . . . meeting with the stranger . . .
who now calls it home.
Why am I here?
What was it . . . calling me?

Then on to town . . .
more old friends . . .
who no longer know . . .

no longer recognize . . . me.
That me who died . . .
yet still remembers . . . them.
Why am I here?
What was it . . . calling me?

And then I see you there . . .
absorbed with your task . . .
Too busy to notice . . . me.
I stand . . . I watch . . .
then call out your name . . . "Mandy."
You look . . . but even you . . .
don't recognize me.
Why am I here?
What was it . . . calling me?

We talk a moment
then your memory clears of me . . .
your one-time friend . . .
your almost lover.
You seem amazed . . .
seem to have trouble believing . . .
that this . . . is really me.
Why am I here?
What was it . . . calling me?

I speak from my heart . . .
about where I'm at . . .
about where I want to be.
Then you . . . in return . . .
And I begin to learn . . .
why it is that I'm here . . .
what it was . . . calling me.
That "me" who I was then
Is no longer the "me" I am now.

For you live with a man
you no longer love . . .
And I can see in your eyes . . .
that you still care . . . for me.
That me who died . . .
That me who can no longer be.
That me from back then. . .
Is the ghost . . .
the me, who is now haunting me.

I do what I came to do.
I give my book to you.
For it tells you of my journey . . .
and invites you to come along . . .
to take your journey too.

For you have stayed here so long . . .
Here . . . where you don't want to be.
Here . . . where I used to be.

And for me . . .
to see where once I worked . . .
as mechanic . . . pump jockey . . . UPS clerk.
Now automated . . . a self-serve . . .
filled in inside . . . on either end.
A Chester Chicken replaces UPS . . .
and Taco Bell is now the area
where I once turned my wrench.
Where that me who was can no longer be.

Yes, for me . . . it all has changed . . .
No longer the same . . .
No longer home . . . my home.
A whoosh of chill air . . . it slams behind . . .
a door now closed . . . forever.
Yes I know why I'm here.
It was me calling me . . .
once more here . . . to say . . .
goodbye.

Moose Milk & Horse Puckies
Chapter 30

Is She the One?

The Whole Life Expo . . .
For some, the experience of airy fairy . . .
For others, the essence of moose milk . . .
Yet others, making the connection
to what lies within . . .
to their heart . . .
to their joy . . .
to their soul.
And for me . . .
I saw what I searched for in her eyes
I heard her in my heart . . .
That spark of recognition
I've seen before . . .
in other women . . .
from other times . . .
in other lives.
Kindred spirits . . .
soul mates I've known before
and recognized . . .
here in this life.

*Yet with her it is more . . .
more than ever before . . .
With her . . .
I can feel it to my core,
as a song . . .
as a dance . . .
This delight that I feel
in her energy field . . .
shouts it clear . . .
shouts it loud . . .
"She is the one! . . .
the woman of my soul!"
My heart sings out with joy
as it joins in the song . . .
of hers.*

A Place Called Loving

I searched for loving
through places I called "right"
yet found others called it "wrong."
And when I went where they said it was,
for me, whatever that was . . . was gone.
So I stopped and looked
where only I could go
to that personal space within
and found what it was
I wanted to know.
Like a river, love is something that flows,
not from anywhere without . . .
love only flows from within.

Loving Mona
Chapter 31
>>> *No poetry written for Chapters 32-33-34* <<<

The One Who Won't Leave

I create my relationships . . .
even created your leaving . . .
by not being there for you,
in love-struck moon-eyed drooling . . .
Searching for what would please you . . .
Trying to "make" you happy.

Perhaps that is my way of searching . . .
Weeding, out those who would leave . . .
Making room for the one who would stay . . .
who finds happiness in being here with me.
Here, only because she wants to be.
That, is the woman with whom I want to be.

Maureen

I met you.
You were special . . . different . . .
an enigma—
Sophisticated in your high-powered
executive world.
Yet a Babe . . . nicely naïve . . . in mine.
Two aliens . . .
meeting at the heart.
I felt the pull . . . the attraction.
Like a magnet, I was drawn to you.
I felt a want of something more,
something permanent.
The ride was like a skydive.
The thrill . . .
the glimpse of far horizons . . .
feeling the speed . . .
falling through the wind
of your expectations
the "who" you wanted me to be,
rushing breathlessly earthward.

And ending abruptly,
with unopened chute . . .
A short burst of pain,
a sudden shift . . .
A change of realities when you said,
"I like you.
And I want to be your friend."
Now strangely . . . I am relieved,
once again . . . to just be me.
Yet I know . . . in my higher mind,
I know . . . everything about you,
and you . . . me.
And my higher mind will always follow
orders from my consciousness.
Why am I still ordering . . .
picking . . . insuring . . .
women who don't want me?
Why did I not pull the ripcord?
Ride in on the wind of your expectations
drop into your life on a lie.
That was not how I wanted it to be.
Is that what you wanted from me?

Florence

Bubbly . . . outgoing . . .
voluptuous Florence....
A mask to hide behind....
a cover for a tender vulnerable heart.
A heart torn unfairly . . .
cruelly ripped apart.
Still bleeding the tears of her anguish.
Silent unseen tears . . .
standing in the window of her life,
forever looking out.
Allowing tracks of dirty shoes,
tracks marring the purity of her house.
Still looking out there for her life.
Yet it is when the sun goes down
and darkness comes around.
When out there the focus fades to black,
then, is when her windows
turn to mirrors.
Then, is when she will look inside . . .
inside her broken heart.

Is there time to clean the carpet
remove the shit stains trampled there
by a loved one's dirty shoes?
Is there time to drain the sorrow
to make room for a new love
on the 'morrow?

Epilogue

Gifts

What is this gift you give to me . . .
Is there something about me you expect me to change?
Or do you perhaps, expect me to do something in return for you?
You Do?
Then this "gift" you "give," is but a chain . . .
A bribe . . . a payment meant only to enslave.
Or, perhaps, to pay me to behave . . .
to live my life . . . your way.
If this "gift" you "gave" was not by request . . .
or in filling a need I could not do,
then it was never your gift to me . . .
It was always your gift to you.
One to be paid for by me.

There's a Wind

There's a wind out there
that I mean to ride,
with a heart that knows but joy inside.
Scents of cedar, sage, and pinion pine,
refreshes that youth still in my mind.
Once more mine . . .

There's mountains, and rivers,
and deserts wide,
where the passions of my soul resides.
Slick rock canyons and cliffs so high,
where one can ride and touch the sky.
Freeing one's soul to fly . . .

Such beauty . . .
all for me to see.
Such joy to know, as I ride free.
And sometime . . . perhaps . . .
There will be you with me.
Me loving you, you loving me.
Both free to be who each wants to be.

An Eagle's Flight—In Poetry

About The Author

Edmond E. Frank a.k.a.
E. Egorhh Frank

When one has experienced and seen the end of one's life, there comes a bottom-line knowing that what is of most importance is to be honest with oneself. This is your life—you only get the one. Are you reaching for the true joys of your heart? Or are you giving yourself away, living your life to suit the wants of others, as society demands. Such knowledge is not taught in any institution. It is a rare and uniquely precious understanding that Ed has, and shares.

Adopted at the age of four, Ed lived a *normal* life for his first forty-five years. As a mechanic, he existed from paycheck to paycheck, just getting by, doing what was expected. It was only with the imminence of death that he finally realized how he was someone he didn't like or respect. Living one's life to please others always has that effect.

Now a Personal Life Coach and writer, he is living proof that we all, at any point in life, can change to become the "who" we really want to be.

Through his writing, he offers change to others. It does not necessarily take meeting the Angel of Death to catalyze change. Unlike with Ed, that angel seldom gives us the gift of a second chance. Ed's novels gives a layman view of how change is done, its price, and of the magnificent adventure found in living the life of one's dreams.

Here are a few facts about Edmond E. Frank, also known to his friends as Egorhh—his middle name—or "Coach Egorhh" to some.

- Majored in Geology at the University of Utah.
- Vietnam era vet—Army honorably discharged.
- Lived some years abroad—Australia, Greece, and Korea.
- A creative artisan, silversmith, and lapidist.
- A committed father and ex-husband.
- A man who has worked through the pain of divorce, lost everything he once thought important in life, and started over

- again, living a life of real importance to his soul.
- Is a poet and author of ten books (currently).
- A man who has done his own healing work.
- He is a Personal Life Coach—Graduate of Coach University & the WeCoach training programs.
- He knows and lives Spiritual Law.
- He is a teacher, mentor, and a servant leader.
- He has volunteered countless hours in self-help seminars supporting others in their growth.
- A man who is familiar with experiential workshops, ropes courses/high wire events,
- Familiar with Reiki, NLP, HPP, Silva and many other forms of meditation.
- Has participated in Native American sweat lodges.
- As is a biker he rode with the American Legion Riders.
- We was the first State Captain for the Nevada Patriot Guard.
- The last twelve years of his working life he served the disabled as a Para Transit bus driver. Seeing first-hand what his clients had to deal with in their lives, was a truly humbling experience.

Coach Egorhh is a man of passion and compassion who knows how, and lives life fully! Bottom line: Ed is one of those, who has learned to love himself. This is the first requirement for having the ability to love others.

He currently resides in Las Vegas, Nevada, and no longer coaches one-on-one in person or over the phone. As a writer and published author, he finds he can reach out and touch many more minds through his books than he ever could as a practicing Personal Life Coach.

This current book is comprised of the poems removed from his second novel *Soul of an Eagle*. Both novels were based on his memoirs. Published back to back with Book Four in his Redneck Spirituality series on spiritual laws (authored under the name E. Egorhh Frank) they may well be his last.

His Redneck Spirituality Series are workbooks meant to be worked. And it's okay if some folks just want to read this, up there, in the bleachers, above the field of life. Not everyone has the courage to play down here on the field—much less acknowledge it as "Rumi's Field." What about you?

The novel these poems were originally used to illustrate is titled *The Soul of an Eagle*. It is the sequel to this author's first work *The Courage of a Butterfly*. Both tell the story fully and in depth. You can order them through Barns and Noble or Amazon. Or, if you have a favorite bookstore they likely can get them for you as well.

NOTE:

Honesty in all my writing is important to me. It is industry standard to have someone else, real or pretended, write about the author in third person—no one likes a braggart. This section is written in the conventional third person format—but in honesty—by me, the author.

As mentioned, I just recently published the sequel novel into which this poetry was originally written. That novel was finished a couple of years earlier. It ended with me and my second wife riding off into the sunset. But I could not bring myself to publish it. It was a lie.

Y'know, a lot of marriages end when one partner cheats or is not who the other wants—both questions of honesty. Neither of us cheated. But in the end I wasn't the person she accepted. It was not a question of anyone's dishonesty, but sadly, of disloyalty. She saw something in our relationship that she believed was "wrong." Truth was, the wrong was only the choice of her perception. I loved her and would still be there but that was no longer a choice for me. It is so much easier to blame others for what one won't even look at concerning one's self. And yet, it WAS in my life and I DID create it.

As for writing the book, I could not face myself if the story of our life together was not the truth. But the truth was distasteful to me—and likely embarrassing to her.

I loved her, but if you want to be with someone it is required that they be acceptable in your mind. Initially that was a struggle for me. But I won my struggle and accepted her without change. Eight years into our relationship she discovered the truth—my truth—about that struggle. The fact that there ever was a struggle made me unacceptable to her.

With a broken heart I released her with love. That is the truth about that book, this book, and my life. I am alone now, and I wonder: Is

there a woman out there who values truth, and has the courage to take responsibility for everything in her life rather than to blame.
Ah, but doesn't our Christian religion give God credit for all that's good shit in our lives, hold Satan responsible for all the evil we do, and blames our significant other for our unhappiness. We have all been taught that we are never the responsible party for anything involving our feelings.

Now I know what the Salmon feels like in swimming upstream just to spawn. Arduous, and always in danger from the jaws of the bear. The bear got me in both my marriages.

But spawning? It is such a wondrous thing. It's more than just the fucking. It's about the companionship—it's about having someone who believes in you and has your back, no matter what. I would like to experience that, just once, before I again meet the Angel of Death.

> *Will it always be,*
> *that the women I love will see . . .*
> *what you now, have taught to me?*
> *Will my love . . .*
> *ever . . .*
> *be "good enough?"*

It never has, although my love has always been true.
I am worthy . . . and so it is.

www.ingramcontent.com/pod-product-compliance
Lightning Source LLC
Chambersburg PA
CBHW030231100526
44583CB00013BA/751